TRINITY AND ALL SAINTS
A COLLEGE OF THE UNIVERSITY OF LEEDS

COLLECTED ANIMAL POEMS VOLUME 3
A March Calf

COLLECTED ANIMAL POEMS

Ted Hughes

COLLECTED ANIMAL POEMS

VOLUME 3

A March Calf

faber and faber

LONDON · BOSTON

First published in Great Britain in 1995
by Faber and Faber Limited
3 Queen Square London WC1N 3AU

Phototypeset by Wilmaset Ltd, Birkenhead, Wirral
Printed in England by Clays Ltd, St Ives plc

A CIP record for this book
is available from the British Library

ISBN 0–571–17625–9 (cased)
    0–571–17626–7 (pbk)

10 9 8 7 6 5 4 3 2 1

to Olwyn and Gerald

Contents

A March Calf

Right from the start he is dressed in his best – his blacks
    and his whites.
Little Fauntleroy – quiffed and glossy,
A Sunday suit, a wedding natty get-up,
Standing in dunged straw

Under cobwebby beams, near the mud wall,
Half of him legs,
Shining-eyed, requiring nothing more
But that mother's milk come back often.

Everything else is in order, just as it is.
Let the summer skies hold off, for the moment.
This is just as he wants it.
A little at a time, of each new thing, is best.

Too much and too sudden is too frightening –
When I block the light, a bulk from space,
To let him in to his mother for a suck,
He bolts a yard or two, then freezes,

Staring from every hair in all directions,
Ready for the worst, shut up in his hopeful religion,
A little syllogism
With a wet blue-reddish muzzle, for God's thumb.

You see all his hopes bustling
As he reaches between the worn rails toward
The top-heavy oven of his mother.
He trembles to grow, stretching his curl-tip tongue –

What did cattle ever find here
To make this dear little fellow
So eager to prepare himself?
He is already in the race, and quivering to win –

His new purpled eyeball swivel-jerks
In the elbowing push of his plans.
Hungry people are getting hungrier,
Butchers developing expertise and markets,

But he just wobbles his tail – and glistens
Within his dapper profile
Unaware of how his whole lineage
Has been tied up.

He shivers for feel of the world licking his side.
He is like an ember – one glow
Of lighting himself up
With the fuel of himself, breathing and brightening.

Soon he'll plunge out, to scatter his seething joy,
To be present at the grass,
To be free on the surface of such a wideness,
To find himself himself. To stand. To moo.

A Swallow

Has slipped through a fracture in the snow-sheet
Which is still our sky –

She flicks past, ahead of her name,
Twinkling away out over the lake.

Reaching this way and that way, with her scissors,
Snipping midges
Trout are still too numb and sunken to stir for.

Sahara clay ovens, at mirage heat,
Glazed her blues, and still she is hot.

She wearied of snatching clegs off the lugs of buffaloes
And of lassooing the flirt-flags of gazelles.

They told her the North was one giant snowball
Rolling South. She did not believe them.
So she exchanged the starry chart of Columbus
For a beggar's bowl of mud.

Setting her compass-tremor tail-needles
She harpooned a wind
That wallowed in the ocean,
Working her barbs deeper
Through that twisting mass she came –

Did she close her eyes and trust in God?
No, she saw lighthouses
Streaming in chaos
Like sparks from a chimney –

She had fixed her instruments on home.

[3]

And now, suddenly, into a blanch-tree stillness
A silence of celandines,
A fringing and stupor of frost,
She bursts, weightless –
                                        to anchor
On eggs frail as frost.

There she goes, flung taut on her leash,
Her eyes at her mouth-corners,
Water-skiing out across a wind
That wrecks great flakes against windscreens.

The Canal's Drowning Black

Bred wild leopards – among the pale depth fungus.
Loach. Torpid, ginger-bearded, secret
Prehistory of the canal's masonry,
With little cupid mouths.

Five inches huge!
On the slime-brink, over bridge reflections,
I teetered. Then a ringing, skull-jolt stamp
And their beards flowered sudden anemones

All down the sunken cliff. A mad-house thrill –
The stonework's tiny eyes, two feet, three feet,
Four feet down through my reflection
Watched for my next move.

Their schooldays were over.
Peeping man was no part of their knowledge.
So when a monkey god, a Martian
Tickled their underchins with his net rim

They snaked out and over the net rim easy
Back into the oligocene –
Only restrained by a mesh of kitchen curtain.
Then flopped out of their ocean-shifting aeons

Into a two-pound jam-jar
On a windowsill
Blackened with acid rain fall-out
From Manchester's rotten lung.

Next morning, Mount Zion's
Cowled, satanic majesty behind me
I lobbed – one by one – high through the air
The stiff, pouting, failed, paled new moons

Back into their Paradise and mine.

Pets

A dark November night, late. The back door wide.
Beyond the doorway, the step off into space.
On the threshold, looking out,
With foxy-furry tail lifted, a kitten.
Somewhere out there, a badger, our lodger,
A stripe-faced rusher at cats, a grim savager,
Is crunching the bones and meat of a hare
Left out for her nightly emergence
From under the outhouses.

The kitten flirts his tail, arches his back –
All his hairs are inquisitive.
Dare he go for a pee?
Something is moving there, just in dark.
A prowling lump. A tabby tom. Grows.
And the battered master of the house
After a month at sea, comes through the doorway,

Recovered from his nearly fatal mauling,
Two probably three pounds heavier
Since that last time he dragged in for help.
He deigns to recognize me
With his criminal eyes, his deformed voice.
Then poises, head lowered, muscle-bound,
Like a bull for the judges,
A thick Devon bull,
Sniffing the celebration of sardines.

Mackerel Song

While others sing the mackerel's armour
His stub scissor head and his big blurred eye
And the flimsy savagery of his onset
I sing his simple hunger.

While others sing the mackerel's swagger
His miniature ocelot oil-green stripings
And his torpedo solidity of thump
I sing his gormless plenty.

While others sing the mackerel's fury
The belly-tug lightning-trickle of his evasions
And the wrist-thick muscle of his last word
I sing his loyal come-back.

While others sing the mackerel's acquaintance
The soap of phosphorus he lathers on your fingers
The midget gut and the tropical racer's torso
I sing his scorched sweetness.

While others sing the mackerel's demise
His ultimatum to be cooked instantly
And the shock of his decay announcement
I sing how he makes the rich summer seas

A billion times richer

With the gift of his billions.

Tigress

She grin-lifts
Her black lips and white whiskers
As she yearns forward

Complaining
Tearing complaint off and banging it down a long pipe
That echoes and hums after

Her stride floats
Enjoying a weightlessness
A near-levitation

Again her cry
Scours out the drum of her

Her face
Works at its lacks and longings and quells
Its angers and rehearses its revenges
Endlessly

She lifts again
The welded and bolted plates of her head
Like an illness past curing

She rolls groaning
A bullet of anguish out of her

She is moving, in her hanging regalia
Everything in her is moving, slipping away forward
From the hindward-taper, drawing herself
Out of the air, like a tail out of water

A bow on the war-path, carrying itself
With its dazzling and painted arrows

Shoulders walling her chest, she goes
Between travelling armed walls

Lifting her brow as she walks to ripple
The surface of the element she moves in

Her cry rips the top off the air first
Then disembowels it

She lies down, as if she were lowering
A great snake into the ground

She rests her head on her forepaws, huge trouble
All her lines too enormous for her

I look into her almond eyes. She frowns
Them shut, the fur moving down on her brows.

Off-Days

In the lowest pit of the solstice, among sour conifers,
The reservoir looked reluctant.
Shrunk low, lying as if ill
Beneath its rusty harness of old waterlines.
Its only life – shivers of patience.

Man-made and officially ugly
Its bed is a desert of black, private depression.
A second whole day we have called for a pike.
Nothing volunteers for election.

If there is one last pike – one old mule,
One last patriot,
It starves, resolutely legless,
Hunger closed,
Habits hardening to total absence
In this grave of spontaneity.

Wind off the lake-face, unexpected blows
Bleak as a knuckle
Is the water's only peevish trick.

We try to imagine our dredging lures
Resurrecting one jerk of life
In the eyeballs
Of mud.

For days somebody's dead herring has lain
Miserably visible,
Like a failed bribe.

Finish!
The pike here
Have been reabsorbed by the outcrop.

All jaws have resumed the Jurassic!

Waterlicked

Bluster-shower August – exploded thunderlight
Tumbling in a crystal.

Eastward an hour, defectors, fishing like truants.

August Bank-Holiday millions roaming in disquiet.

A thought of pike, thoroughly ravenous,
In Bridgewater canal. Woe on the hope!

Flow-combed pond-weed folded the dull water
In a sunk hammock, where our plug-baits garishly
    popped.

All afternoon, with between-cloud glare, and the long
    hurt
Of the bent narrows. A weariness wore us.

A thin madness of windy-glitter water and its empty
    fractures.

All afternoon, Esox inert subombra
Like a fixed eternal number, ferocious and lucid.
Absent as baby's dreams.
                    In a migraine of dazzle and gloom
We flitted away Westward, among spark emeralds,
To the blue twilit lintel.

Mosquito

To get into life
Mosquito died many deaths.

The slow millstone of polar ice, turned by the galaxy,
Only polished her egg.

Sub-zero, bulging all its mountain-power,
Failed to fracture her bubble.

The lake that squeezed her kneeled,
Tightened to granite – splintering quartz teeth,
But only sharpened her needle.

Till the strain was too much, even for Earth.

The stars drew off, trembling.
The mountains sat back, sweating.

The lake burst.

Mosquito

Flew up singing, over the broken waters –

A little haze of wings, a midget sun.

Sheep

The sheep has stopped crying.
All morning in her wire-mesh compound
On the lawn, she has been crying
For her vanished lamb. Yesterday they came.
Then her lamb could stand, in a fashion,
And make some tiptoe cringing steps.
Now he has disappeared.
He was only half the proper size,
And his cry was wrong. It was not
A dry little hard bleat, a baby-cry
Over a flat tongue, it was human,
It was a despairing human smooth Oh!
Like no lamb I ever heard. Its hind legs
Cowered in under its lumped spine,
Its feeble hips leaned towards
Its shoulders for support. Its stubby
White wool pyramid head, on a tottery neck,
Had sad and defeated eyes, pinched, pathetic,
Too small, and it cried all the time
Oh! Oh! staggering towards
Its alert, baffled, stamping, storming mother
Who feared our intentions. He was too weak
To find her teats, or to nuzzle up in under,
He hadn't the gumption. He was fully
Occupied just standing, then shuffling
Towards where she'd removed to. She knew
He wasn't right, she couldn't
Make him out. Then his rough-curl legs,
So stoutly built, and hooved
With real quality tips,

Just got in the way, like a loose bundle
Of firewood he was cursed to manage,
Too heavy for him, lending sometimes
Some support, but no strength, no real help.
When we sat his mother on her tail, he mouthed her
    teat,
Slobbered a little, but after a minute
Lost aim and interest, his muzzle wandered,
He was managing a difficulty
Much more urgent and important. By evening
He could not stand. It was not
That he could not thrive, he was born
With everything but the will –
That can be deformed, just like a limb.
Death was more interesting to him.
Life could not get his attention.
So he died, with the yellow birth-mucus
Still in his cardigan.
He did not survive a warm summer night.
Now his mother has started crying again.
The wind is oceanic in the elms
And the blossom is all set.

II

What is it this time the dark barn again
Where men jerk me off my feet
And shout over me with murder voices
And do something painful to somewhere on my body

Why am I grabbed by the leg and dragged from my
    friends
Where I was hidden safe though it was hot
Why am I dragged into the light and whirled onto my
    back
Why am I sat up on my rear end with my legs splayed

A man grips me helpless his knees grip me helpless
What is that buzzer what is it coming
Buzzing like a big fierce insect on a long tangling of
    snake
What is the man doing to me with his buzzing thing

That I cannot see he is pressing it into me
I surrender I let my legs kick I let myself be killed

I let him hoist me about he twists me flat
In a leverage of arms and legs my neck pinned under his
    ankle

While he does something dreadful down the whole
    length of my belly
My little teats stand helpless and terrified as he buzzes
    around them

Poor old ewe! She peers around from her ridiculous
    position.
Cool intelligent eyes, of grey-banded agate and amber,

Eyes deep and clear with feeling and understanding
While her monster hooves dangle helpless
And a groan like no bleat vibrates in her squashed
    windpipe
And the cutter buzzes at her groin and her fleece piles
    away

Now it buzzes at her throat and she emerges whitely
More and more grotesquely female and nude
Paunchy and skinny, while her old rug, with its foul
    tassels
Heaps from her as a foam-stiff, foam-soft, yolk-yellow
    robe

Numbed all over she suddenly feels much lighter
She feels herself free, her legs are her own and she scrambles
    up
Waiting for that grapple of hands to fling her down again
She stands in the opened arch of his knees she is facing a
    bright doorway

With a real bleat to comfort the lamb in herself
She trots across the threshold and makes one high clearing
    bound
To break from the cramp of her fright
And surprised by her new lightness and delighted

She trots away, noble-nosed, her pride unsmirched.
Her greasy winter-weight stays coiled on the foul floor,
    for somebody else to bother about.
She has a beautiful wet green brand on her bobbing
    brand-new backside,
She baas, she has come off best.

III

The mothers have come back
From the shearing, and behind the hedge
The woe of sheep is like a battlefield
In the evening, when the fighting is over,
And the cold begins, and the dew falls,
And bowed women move with water.

Mother mother mother the lambs
Are crying, and the mothers are crying.
Nothing can resist that probe, that cry
Of a lamb for its mother, or an ewe's crying
For its lamb. The lambs cannot find
Their mothers among those shorn strangers.
A half-hour they have lamented,
Shaking their voices in desperation.
Bald brutal-voiced mothers braying out,
Flat-tongued lambs chopping off hopelessness.
Their hearts are in panic, their bodies
Are a mess of woe, woe they cry,
They mingle their trouble, a music
Of worse and worse distress, a worse entangling,
They hurry out little notes
With all their strength, cries searching this way and that.
The mothers force out sudden despair, blaaa!
On restless feet, with wild heads.

Their anguish goes on and on, in the June heat.
Only slowly their hurt dies, cry by cry,
As they fit themselves to what has happened.

Sparrow

The strike drags on. With the other idle hands
He draws dole. The sun is a dusty cinder.
Gold-haze afternoon muffles their shouts
Scuffling over a tossed coin, on the allotments.

Shut in his elder bush, he's a drab artist –
He chisels a pebble,
Or swites and scrapes at a stub-whistle
With a worn little penknife.

Suddenly flings it all down, furious,
And joins the gang-scrimmage.
A flustery hen-bird with her knickers torn
Tries to escape through the rhubarb.

Pin-legged urchin, he's patient.
He bathes in smoke. He towels in soot,
And with his prematurely-aged hungry street-cry
Sells his consumptive sister.

Or he swirls to the stackyard –
A thrown handful of him and his family –
Seed and chaff together –
The country air is good. It carves him afresh

Out of a ripely-grained chunk of dark oak.

Or he rests, face of a senile mouse,
Odysseus just back, penniless,
Burned out with African adventure,
Picking up how to beg.

The Long Tunnel Ceiling

Of the main road canal bridge
Cradled black stalactite reflections.
That was the place for dark loach!

At the far end, the Moderna blanket factory
And the bushy mask of Hathershelf above it
Peered in through the cell-window.

Lorries from Bradford, baled with plump and towering
Wools and cottons met, just over my head,
Lorries from Rochdale, and ground past each other
Making that cavern of air and water tremble –

Suddenly a crash!
The long gleam-ponderous watery echo shattered.

And at last it had begun!
That could only have been a brick from the ceiling!
The bridge was starting to collapse!

But the canal swallowed its scare,
The heavy mirror reglassed itself,
And the black arch gazed up at the black arch.

Till a brick
Rose through its eruption – hung massive
Then slammed back with a shock and a shattering.

An ingot!
Holy of holies! A treasure!
A trout
Nearly as long as my arm, solid
Molten pig of many a bronze loach!

There he lay – lazy – a free lord,
Ignoring me. Caressing, dismissing
The eastward easing traffic of drift,
Master of the Pennine Pass!

Found in some thin glitter among mean sandstone,
High under ferns, high up near sour heather,

Brought down on a midnight cloudburst
In a shake-up of heaven and the hills
When the streams split with zig-zags and explosions

A seed
Of the wild god now flowering for me,
Such a tigerish, dark, breathing lily
Between the tyres, under the tortured axles.

Song against the White Owl

The white owl got its proof weapons
Bequests of its victims.

And it got those eyes that look beyond life
From fluorescence of old corpses.

It snatched its bones as it could
From the burnings of blizzard.

Death loaned it a belly.
It wears a face it found on the sea.

Twisting sinews of last breaths
It bent these oddments together.

With a ghostly needle of screech
It sewed a coat of the snow

From the knobbed and staring ice
Wringing blood and fat.

O stare Owl stare
Through your glacier wall
At a fatal terrain
Of weeping snow and the leaf of the birch

Where I spoon your soul from a bowl
And my song steams.

Teaching a Dumb Calf

She came in reluctant. The dark shed
Was too webby with reminiscences, none pleasant,
And she would not go in. She swung away,
Rolled her tug belly in the oily sway of her legs.
Deep and straw-foul the mud. Leakage green
From earlier occupants, fermenting. I tried
To lift her calf in ahead of her, a stocky red block,
And she pacific drove her head at me,
Light-nimble as a fist, bullied me off,
And swung away, calling her picky-footed boy
And pulling for the open field, the far beeches
In their fly-green emerald leaf of a day.
We shooed and shouted her back, and I tried again
Pulling the calf from among her legs, but it collapsed
Its hind legs and lay doggo, in the abominable mud,
And her twisting hard head, heavier than a shoulder,
Butted me off. And again she swung away.
Then I picked her calf up bodily and went in.
Little piggy eyes, she followed me. Then I roped her,
And drew her to the head of the stall, tightened her
Hard to the oak pillar, with her nose in the hay-rack,
And she choke-bellowed query comfort to herself.
He was trying to suck – but lacked the savvy.
He didn't get his nape down dipped enough
Or his nose craning tongue upward enough
Under her tight hard bag of stiff teats each
The size of a labrador's muzzle. They were too big.
He nuzzled slobbering at their fat sides
But couldn't bring one in. They were dripping,
And as he excited them they started squirting.
I fumbled one into his mouth – I had to hold it,

Stuffing its slippery muscle into his suction,
His rim-teeth and working tongue. He preferred
The edge of my milk-lathered hand, easier dimension,
But he got going finally, all his new
Machinery learning suddenly, and she stilled,
Mooing indignity, rolling her red rims,
Till the happy warm peace gathered them
Into its ancient statue.

Cuckoo

Away, Cuckoo!
                    That first cry in April
Taps at the blood suspended
In its ponderous jar
Like a finger-tip at a barometer.

That first ribald whoop, like a stolen kiss
Sets the month trembling. The orchard flushes
And the hairy copse grows faint with bluebells.

Sudden popping up of a lolling Priapus –
Hooha! Hooha!
Dizzying Milkymaids with innuendo.

Cuckoo jinks in – dowses his hawk-fright crucifix
Over the nest-bird's eye
And leaves his shadow in the egg.

Then his cry flees guilty, hill to hollow,
Hunted by itself, all day dodging
The dropped double that dogs it.

O orphan of orphans! O moon-witted
Ill-bred dud-hawk,
Cavorting on pylons, you and your witchy moll.

With heartless blow on blow, all afternoon,
You open hair-fine fractures through the precarious
Porcelain hearts of spinsters in rose cottages.

Yet progress through the shire, April hazy,
With some stateliness – like a day comet
Trailing a vista-shimmering shawl of echoes

As you duck under gates, pursued by a husband,
Covering your tracks, two of you, three, ventriloqual –
Over the hill, in the wood, and in the egg.

Seven weeks. Eight. Then you and your wife sit cackling,
Chuckling, hiccuping, syncopating
Your lewd loopy shout

Into a ghoulish, stuttering,
Double-act
Gag about baby-murder.

                    Away, Cuckoo!

Visitation

All night the river's twists
Bit each other's tails, in happy play.

Suddenly a dark other
Twisted among them.

And a cry, half sky, half bird,
Slithered over roots.
                    A star
Fleetingly etched it.
                    Dawn
Puzzles a sunk branch under deep tremblings.

Nettles will not tell.
                    Who shall say

That the river
Crawled out of the river, and whistled,
And was answered by another river?

A strange tree
Is the water of life –

Sheds these pad-clusters on mud-margins
One dawn in a year, her eeriest flower.

Under the Hill of Centurions

The river is in a resurrection fever.
Now at Easter you find them
Up in the pool's throat, and in the very jugular
Where the stickle pulses under grasses –

Cock minnows!

They have abandoned contemplation and prayer in the
   pool's crypt.

There they are, packed all together,
In an inch of seething light.

A stag-party, all bridegrooms, all in their panoply –

Red-breasted as if they bled, their Roman
Bottle-glass greened bodies silked with black

In the clatter of the light loom of water,
All singing and
Toiling together,
Wreathing their metals
Into the warp and weft of the lit water –

I imagine their song,
Deep-chested, striving, solemn.

A wrestling tress of kingfisher colour,
Steely jostlings, a washed mass of brilliants

Labouring at earth
In the wheel of light –

Ghostly rinsings
A struggle of spirits.

Eclipse

For half an hour, through a magnifying glass,
I've watched the spiders making love undisturbed,
Ignorant of the voyeur, horribly happy.

First in the lower left-hand corner of the window
I saw an average spider stirring. There
In a midden of carcases, the shambles
Of insects dried in their colours,
A trophy den of uniforms, reds, greens,
Yellow-striped and detached wing-frails, last year's
Leavings, parched a winter, scentless – heads,
Bodices, corsets, leg-shells, a crumble of shards
In a museum of dust and neglect, there
In the crevice, concealed by corpses in their old
    wrappings,
A spider has come to live. She has spun
An untidy nearly invisible
Floss of strands, a few aimless angles
Camouflaged as the grey dirt of the rain-stains
On the glass. I saw her moving. Then a smaller,
Just as ginger, similar all over,
Only smaller. He had suddenly appeared.

Upside down, she was doing a gentle
Sinister dance. All legs clinging
Except for those leading two, which tapped on the web,
Trembling it, I thought, like a fly, to attract
The immobile, upside-down male, near the frame,
Only an inch from her. He moved away,
Turning ready to flee, I guessed. Maybe
Fearful of her intentions and appetites:
Doubting. But her power, focusing,

Making no error after the millions of years
Perfecting this art, turned him round
At a distance of two inches, and hung him
Upside down, head under, belly towards her.
Motionless, except for a faint
And just-detectable throb of his hair-leg tips.
She came closer, upside down, gently,
And enmeshed his forelegs in hers.

So, I imagined, here is the famous murder.
I got closer to watch. Something
Difficult to understand, difficult
To properly observe was going on.
Her two hands seemed swollen, like tiny crab-claws.
Those two nippers she folds up under nose
To bring things to her pincers, they were moving,
Glistening. He convulsed now and again.
Her abdomen pod twitched – spasmed slightly
Little mean ecstasies. Was she pulling him to pieces?
Something much more delicate, a much more
Delicate agreement was in process.
Under his abdomen he had a nozzle –
Presumably his lumpy little cock,
Just as ginger as the rest of him, a teat,
An infinitesimal nipple. Probably
Under a microscope it is tooled and designed
Like some micro-device in a space rocket.
To me it looked crude and simple. Far from simple,
Though, were her palps, her boxing-glove nippers –
They were like the mechanical hands
That manipulate radioactive matter
On the other side of safe screen glass.
But hideously dexterous. She reached out one,

I cannot imagine how she saw to do it,
And brought monkey-fingers from under her crab-
   nippers
And grasped his nipple cock. As soon as she had it
A bubble of glisteny clear glue
Ballooned up from her nipper, the size of her head,
Then shrank back, and as it shrank back
She wrenched her grip off his cock
As if it had locked there, and doubled her fistful
Of shining wet to her jaw-pincers
And rubbed her mouth and underskin with it,
Six, seven stiff rubs, while her abdomen twitched,
Her tail-tip flirted, and he hung passive.
Then out came her other clutcher, on its elbow,
And grabbed his bud, and the gloy-thick bubble
Swelled above her claws, a red spur flicked
Inside it, and he jerked in his ropes.
Then the bubble shrank and she twisted it off
And brought it back to stuff her face-place
With whatever it was. Very still,
Except for those stealths and those twitchings
They hung upside down, face to face,
Holding forelegs. It was still obscure
Just what was going on. It went on.
Half an hour. Finally she backed off.
He hung like a dead spider, just as he'd hung
All the time she'd dealt with him.

I thought it must be over. So now, I thought,
I see the murder. I could imagine now
If he stirred she'd think he was a fly,
And she'd be feeling ravenous. And so far
She'd shown small excitement about him

With all that concentration on his attachment,
As if he upside down were just the table
Holding the delicacy. She moved off.
Aimlessly awhile she moved round,
Till I realized she was concentrating
On a V of dusty white, a delta
Of floss that seemed just fuzz. Then I could see
How she danced her belly low in the V.
I saw her fitting, with accurate whisker-fine feet,
Blobs of glue to the fibres, and sticking others
To thicken and deepen the V, and knot its juncture.
Then she danced in place, belly down, on this –
Suddenly got up and hung herself
Over the V. Sitting in the cup of the V
Was a tiny blob of new whiteness.
A first egg? Already? Then very carefully
She dabbed at the blob, and worked more woolly fibres
Into the V, to either side of it,
Diminishing it as she dabbed. I could see
I was watching mighty nature
In a purposeful mood, but not what she worked at.
Soon, the little shapeless dot of white
Was a dreg of speck, and she left it. She returned
Towards her male, who hung still in position.
She paused and laboriously cleaned her hands,
Wringing them in her pincers. And suddenly
With a swift, miraculously-accurate snatch
Took something from her mouth, and dumped it
On an outermost cross-strand of web –
A tiny scrap of white – refuse, I thought,
From their lovemaking. So I stopped watching.
Ten minutes later they were at it again.
Now they have vanished. I have scrutinized

The whole rubbish tip of carcases
And the window-frame crannies beneath it.
They are hidden. Is she devouring him now?
Or are there still some days of bliss to come
Before he joins her antiques? They are hidden
Probably together in the fusty dark,
Holding forearms, listening to the rain, rejoicing
As the sun's edge, behind the clouds,
Comes clear of our shadow.

Swans

Washed in Arctic,
Return to their ballroom of glass
Still in the grip of the wizard,

With the jewel stuck in their throats.

Each one still condemned
To meditate all day on her mirror
Hypnotized with awe.

Each swan glued in her reflection
Airy
As the water-caught plume of a swan.

Each snowdrop lyrical daughter possessed
By the coil
Of a black and scowling serpent –

Dipping her eyes into subzero darkness,
Searching the dregs of old lakes
For her lost music.

Then they all writhe up the air,
A hard-hooved onset of cavalry –
Harp the iceberg wall with soft fingers.

Or drift, at evening, far out
Beyond islands, where the burning levels
Spill into the sun

And the snowflake of their enchantment melts.

Feeding Out-Wintering Cattle at Twilight

The wind is inside the hill.
The wood is a struggle – like a wood
Struggling through a wood. A panic
Only just holds off – every gust
Breaches the sky-walls and it seems, this time,
The whole sea of air will pour through,
The thunder will take deep hold, roots
Will have to come out, every loose thing
Will have to lift and go. And the cows, dark lumps of
    dusk
Stand waiting, like nails in a tin roof.
For the crucial moment, taking the strain
In their stirring stillness. As if their hooves
Held their field in place, held the hill
To its trembling shape. Night-thickness
Purples in the turmoil, making
Everything more alarming. Unidentifiable, tiny
Birds go past like elf-bolts.
Battling the hay-bales from me, the cows
Jostle and crush, like hulls blown from their moorings
And piling at the jetty. The wind
Has got inside their wintry buffalo skins,
Their wild woolly bulk-heads, their fierce, joyful
    breathings
And the reckless strength of their necks.
What do they care, their hooves
Are knee-deep in porage of earth –
The hay blows luminous tatters from their chewings,
A fiery loss, frittering downwind,
Snatched away over the near edge
Where the world becomes water

Thundering like a flood-river at night.
They grunt happily, half-dissolved
On their steep, hurtling brink, as I flounder back
Towards headlights.

Black-Back Gull

Tide sighs and turns over. The black-backed gull
Capers from his yoga-sleep
On the far sand-shine. Reality touched him.

The brain-flaying sea-storm's
Old brain wakes up. You see a sun-splinter crystal,
Sharpening clear, lift off inland.

Sea can stay, lazy, sipping
Among mussels. The black-backed gull mounts earth
And crests inland, over his eye's depth,

Bending against wind with the mask-stiff
Solemnity of a mouth
God is trying to speak through.

From a sunken echo-tomb of iron
All the drowned
Gargle over his tongue –

Water, stone, wind, almost spoke.

Dispersing, he whisps frailly along
The sand-hills. Opens the lamb's parcel,
Finds a caring home

For the cow's afterbirth. Collects
What has slipped from human finger-bones
Into the town dump.

The sea's wings, black-backed,
Caress the earth. And a cliff-wheel of wind
Is the playground

Where a salt god laughs. Vomits his laughter
And gulps it back in
Like intestines hanging from the mouth.

Stealing Trout on a May Morning

I park the car half in the ditch and switch off and sit.
The hot astonishment of my engine's arrival
Sinks through 5 a.m. silence and frost.
At the end of a long gash
An atrocity through the lace of first light
I sit with the reeking instrument.
I am on delicate business.
I want the steel to be cold instantly
And myself secreted three fields away
And the farms, back under their blankets, supposing a
    plane passed.

Because this is no wilderness you can just rip into.
Every leaf is plump and well-married,
Every grain of soil of known lineage, well-connected.
And the gardens are like brides fallen asleep
Before their weddings have properly begun.
The orchards are the hushed maids, fresh from convent –
It is too hushed, something improper is going to happen.
It is too ghostly proper, all sorts of liveried listenings
Tiptoe along the lanes and peer over hedges.

I listen for the eyes jerked open on pillows,
Their dreams washed with sudden ugly petroleum.
They need only look out at a sheep.
Every sheep within two miles
Is nailing me accurately down
With its hellishly shaven starved-priest expression.

I emerge. The air, after all, has forgotten everything.
The sugared spindles and wings of grass
Are etched on great goblets. A pigeon falls into space.

The earth is coming quietly and darkly up from a great
   depth,
Still under the surface. I am unknown,
But nothing is surprised. The tarmac of the road
Is velvet with sleep, the hills are out cold.
A new earth still in its wrappers
Of gauze and cellophane,
The frost from the storage still on its edges,
My privilege to poke and sniff.
The sheep are not much more than the primroses.
And the river there, amazed with itself,
Flexing and trying its lights
And unused fish, that are rising
And sinking for the sheer novelty
As the sun melts the hill's spine and the spilled light
Flows through their gills . . .

My mind sinks, rising and sinking.
And the opening arms of the sky forget me
Into the buried tunnels of hazels. There
My boot dangles down, till a thing black and sudden
Savages it, and the river is heaping under,
Alive and malevolent,
A coiling glider of shock, the space-black
Draining off the night-moor, under the hazels –
But I drop and stand square in it, against it,
Then it is river again, washing its soul,
Its stones, its weeds, its fish, its gravels
And the rooty mouths of the hazels clear
Of the discolourings bled in
Off ploughlands and lanes . . .

At first, I can hardly look at it –
The riding tables, the corrugated
Shanty roofs tightening
To braids, boilings where boulders throw up
Gestures of explosion, black splitting everywhere
To drowning skirts of whiteness, a slither of mirrors
Under the wading hazels. Here it is shallow,
Ropes my knees, lobbing fake boomerangs,
A drowned woman loving each ankle,
But I'm heavier and I wade with them upstream,
Flashing my green minnow
Up the open throats of water
And across through the side of the rush
Of alligator escaping along there
Under the beards of the hazels, and I slice
The wild nape-hair off the bald bulges,
Till the tightrope of my first footholds
Tangles away downstream
And my bootsoles move as to magnets.

Soon I deepen. And now I meet the piling mob
Of voices and hurriers coming towards me
And tumbling past me. I press through a panic –
This headlong river is a rout
Of tumbrils and gun-carriages, rags and metal,
All the funeral woe-drag of some overnight disaster
Mixed with planets, electrical storms and darkness
On a mapless moorland of granite,
Trailing past me with all its frights, its eyes
With what they have seen and still see,
They drag the flag off my head, a dark insistence
Tearing the spirits from my mind's edge and from
     under . . .

To yank me clear takes the sudden, strong spine
Of one of the river's real members –
Thoroughly made of dew, lightning and granite
Very slowly over four years. A trout, a foot long,
Lifting its head in a shawl of water,
Fins banked stiff like a schooner
It forces the final curve wide, getting
A long look at me. So much for the horror:
It has changed places.
                    Now I am a man in a painting
(Under the mangy, stuffed head of a fox)
Painted about 1905
Where the river steams and the frost relaxes
On the pear-blossoms. The brassy wood-pigeons
Bubble their colourful voices, and the sun
Rises upon a world well-tried and old.

Where I Sit Writing My Letter

Suddenly hooligan baby starlings
Rain all round me squealing,
Shouting how it's tremendous and everybody
Has to join in and they're off this minute!

Probably the weird aniseed corpse-odour
Of the hawthorn flower's disturbed them,
As it disturbs me. Now they all rise
Flutter-floating, oddly eddying,

Squalling their dry gargles. Then, mad, they
Hurl off, on a new wrench of excitement,
Leaving me out.
                               I pluck apple-blossom,
Cool, blood-lipped, wet open.

And I'm just quieting thoughts towards my letter
When they all come storming back,
Giddy with hoarse hissings and snarls
And clot the top of an ash sapling –

Sizzling bodies, snaky black necks craning
For a fresh thrill – Where next? Where now? Where? – they're
    off
All rushing after it
Leaving me fevered, and addled.

They can't believe their wings.

Snow-bright clouds boil up.

Bringing in New Couples

Wind out of freezing Europe. A mean snow
Fiery cold. Ewes caked crusty with snow,
Their new hot lambs wet trembling
And crying on trampled patches, under the hedge –
Twenty miles of open lower landscape
Blows into their wetness. The field smokes and writhes
Burning like a moor with snow-fumes.
Lambs nestling to make themselves comfortable
While the ewe nudges and nibbles at them
And the numbing snow-wind blows on the blood tatters
At her breached back-end.
The moor a grey sea-shape. The wood
Thick-fingered density, a worked wall of whiteness.
The old sea-roar, sheep-shout, lamb-wail.
Redwings needling invisible. A fright
Smoking among trees, the hedges blocked.
Lifting of ice-heavy ewes, trampling anxieties
As they follow their wide-legged tall lambs,
Tripods craning to cry bewildered.
We coax the mothers to follow their babies
And they do follow, running back
In sudden convinced panic to the patch
Where the lamb had been born, dreading
She must have been deceived away from it
By crafty wolvish humans, then coming again
Defenceless to the bleat she's attuned to
And recognizing her own – a familiar
Detail in the meaningless shape-mass
Of human arms, legs, body-clothes – her lamb on the white
    earth
Held by those hands. Then vanishing again

Lifted. Then only the disembodied cry
Going with the human, while she runs in a circle
On the leash of the cry. While the wind
Presses outer space into the grass
And alarms wrens deep in brambles
With hissing fragments of stars.

Shrike

The talons close amicably
Round the accused
And her pipe of cry.

The dispute is appeased
In a ruffling of comfort,
A cleaning of face-knives.

Shrike, painted for war
And recognition
Digests his fame.

His law, lunar and songless,
Rounds his gaze, a two-lidded eclipse
Of crater silence.

One end of the world!

The sun's justice.

A jury of cadavers.

Caddis

Struggle-drudge – with the ideas of a crocodile
And the physique of a foetus.

Absurd mudlark – living your hovel's life –
Yourself your own worst obstacle.

Lugging Castle Paranoia
Through that moonland, like a train off its track,

Under the river's hurricane.
You should have been a crab. It's no good.

Trout in March are crammed
With the debris of your hopeful redoubts.

Wasp-face, orphaned and a waif too early,
Improvising – with inaudible war-cries –

This Herculean makeshift, hoisting your house,
You can nip my finger but

You are still a baby.
Your alfresco Samurai suit of straws,

Your Nibelungen mail of agates, affirms
Only fantasies of fear and famine.

Hurry up. Join the love-orgy
Up here among leaves, in the light rain,

Under a flimsy tent of dusky wings.

Struggle

We had been expecting her to calve
And there she was, just after dawn, down.
Private, behind bushed hedge-cuttings, in a low rough
   corner.
The walk towards her was like a walk into danger,
Caught by her first calf, the small-boned black and white
   heifer
Having a bad time. She lifted her head,
She reached for us with a wild, flinging look
And flopped flat again. There was the calf,
White-faced, lion-coloured, enormous, trapped
Round the waist by his mother's purpled elastic,
His heavy long forelegs limply bent in a not-yet-inherited
   gallop,
His head curving up and back, pushing for the udder
Which had not yet appeared, his nose scratched and
   reddened
By an ill-placed clump of bitten-off rushes,
His fur dried as if he had been
Half-born for hours, as he probably had.
Then we heaved on his forelegs,
And on his neck, and half-born he mooed
Protesting about everything. Then bending him down,
Between her legs, and sliding a hand
Into the hot tunnel, trying to ease
His sharp hip-bones past her pelvis,
Then twisting him down, so you expected
His spine to slip its sockets,
And one hauling his legs, and one embracing his wet
   waist
Like pulling somebody anyhow from a bog,
And one with hands easing his hips past the corners

Of his tunnel mother, till something gave.
The cow flung her head and lifted her upper hind leg
With every heave, and something gave
Almost a click –
And his scrubbed wet enormous flanks came sliding out,
Coloured ready for the light his incredibly long hind legs
From the loose red flapping sack-mouth
Followed by a gush of colours, a mess
Of puddled tissues and jellies.
He mooed feebly and lay like a pieta Christ
In the cold easterly daylight. We dragged him
Under his mother's nose, her stretched-out exhausted
    head,
So she could get to know him with lickings.
They lay face to face like two mortally wounded duellists.
We stood back, letting the strength flow towards them.
We gave her a drink, we gave her hay. The calf
Started his convalescence
From the gruelling journey. All day he lay
Overpowered by limpness and weight.
We poured his mother's milk into him
But he had not strength to swallow.
He made a few clumsy throat gulps, then lay
Mastering just breathing.
We took him inside. We tucked him up
In front of a stove, and tried to pour
Warm milk and whisky down his throat and not into his
    lungs.
But his eye just lay suffering the monstrous weight of his
    head,
The impossible job of his marvellous huge limbs.
He could not make it. He died called Struggle.
Son of Patience.

Snipe

You are soaked with the cold rain –
Like a pelt in tanning liquor.
The moor's swollen waterbelly
Swags and quivers, ready to burst at a step.

Suddenly
Some scrap of dried fabric rips
Itself up
From the marsh-quake, scattering. A soft

Explosion of twilight
In the eyes, with a spinning fragment
Somewhere. Nearly lost, wing-flash

Stab-trying escape routes, wincing
From each, ducking under
And flinging up over –

Bowed head, jockey shoulders
Climbing headlong
As if hurled downwards –

A mote in the watery eye of the moor –

Hits cloud and
Skis down the far rain wall

Slashes a wet rent
In the rain-dusk
Twisting out sideways –

                        rushes his alarm
Back to the ice-age.

                    The downpour helmet

Tightens on your skull, riddling the pools,
Washing the standing stones and fallen shales
With empty nightfall.

Live Skull

In the lake, behind the mirror

The Pike, a megalith.
Under the flame-flutter
Complexion of water.

The Pike, a sunk lintel
Balanced on stones
Under the crawling nape of light.

The Pike
Non-participant
Under the lake's slow lungs.

The Pike that has somehow, unmoving,
Sailed out of the sun

Into this measured hole –
Cold
A finger

Of the silence of space –
Slow
A smile

Of the deafness of earth

Making the skull creak.

Nightingale

This crack-brained African priest creates his own temple
  ruins
With his cry, with his sacred blade
Rending the veils, opening the throb of God.

Pale Spaniard, your throat thick with death,
Your blood is out of date. The lilac bush
Is no longer the Lord's torture chamber.

Let rip! Sing the score of the stars,
Crash your timbrel hung with negative particles,
Twang the bone guitar of protein!

Your lightning and thunderclap night-voice
Shuts back, with gaggings and splutters,
Into a nun's illuminated book.

And by day you do not exist.

Dehorning

Bad-tempered bullying bunch, the horned cows
Among the unhorned. Feared, spoilt.
Cantankerous at the hay, at assemblies, at crowded
Yard operations. Knowing their horn-tips' position
To a fraction, every other cow knowing it too,
Like their own tenderness. Horning of bellies, hair-
    tufting
Of horn-tips. Handy levers. But
Off with the horns.
So there they all are in the yard –
The pick of the bullies, churning each other
Like thick fish in a bucket, churning their mud.
One by one, into the cage of the crush: the needle,
A roar not like a cow – more like a tiger,
Blast of air down a cavern, and long, long
Beginning in pain and ending in terror – then the next.
The needle between the horn and the eye, so deep
Your gut squirms for the eyeball twisting
In its pink-white fastenings of tissue. This side and that.
Then the first one anaesthetized, back in the crush.
The bulldog pincers in the septum, stretched full
    strength,
The horn levered right over, the chin pulled round
With the pincers, the mouth drooling, the eye
Like a live eye caught in a pan, like the eye of a fish
Imprisoned in air. Then the cheese cutter
Of braided wire, and stainless steel peg handles,
Aligned on the hair-bedded root of the horn, then
    leaning
Backward full weight, pull-punching backwards,
Left right left right and the blood leaks

Down over the cheekbone, the wire bites
And buzzes, the ammonia horn-burn smokes
And the cow groans, roars shapelessly, hurls
Its half-ton commotion in the tight cage. Our faces
Grimace like faces in the dentist's chair. The horn
Rocks from its roots, the wire pulls through
The last hinge of hair, the horn is heavy and free,
And the water-pistol jet of blood
Rains over the one who holds it – a needle jet
From the white-rasped and bloody skull-crater. Then
    tweezers
Twiddle the artery nozzle, knotting it enough,
And purple antiseptic squirts a cuttlefish cloud over it.
Then the other side the same. We collect
A heap of horns. The floor of the crush
Is a trampled puddle of scarlet. The purple-crowned
    cattle,
The bullies, with suddenly no horns to fear,
Start ramming and wrestling. Maybe their heads
Are still anaesthetized. A new order
Among the hornless. The bitchy high-headed
Straight-back brindle, with her Spanish bull trot,
And her head-shaking snorting advance and her crazy
    spirit,
Will have to get maternal. What she's lost
In weapons, she'll have to make up for in tits.
But they've all lost one third of their beauty.

Strangers

Dawn. The river thins.
The combed-out coiffure at the pool-tail
Brightens thinly.
The slung pool's long hammock still flat out.

The sea-trout, a salt flotilla, at anchor,
Substanceless, flame-shadowed,
Hang in a near emptiness of sunlight.

There they actually are, under homebody oaks,
Close to teddybear sheep, near purple loose-strife –

Space-helms bowed in preoccupation,
Only a slight riffling of their tail-ailerons
Corrective of drift,
Gills easing.

And the pool's toiled rampart roots,
The cavorting of new heifers, water-skeeters
On their abacus, even the slow claim
Of the buzzard's hand
Merely decorate a heaven

Where the sea-trout, fixed and pouring,
Lean in the speed of light.
                              They make nothing
Of the strafed hogweed sentry skeletons,
Nothing of the sun, so openly aiming down.

Thistle-floss bowls over them. First, lost leaves
Feel over them with blind shadows.

The sea-trout, upstaring, in trance,
Absorb everything and forget it
Into a blank of bliss.

And this is the real Samadhi – worldless, levitated.

Till, bulging, a man-shape
Wobbles their firmament.
                              Now see the holy ones
Shrink their auras, slim, sink, focus, prepare
To scram like trout.

Mallard

Gloom-glossy wind
Ransacking summer's end. Everything

Suddenly rubbish. Trees
Trying to take off.

Crammed, churned leaf-mass.
The river's shutters clatter.

Myself mixed with it
Inextricably. Blown
Inside out, clinging to my straws,

Gusty skeleton.

Horizons rolling up. Space-witch – sky
Mussel-blue, in a fling of foul skirts,
Gapes a light-streak.
                                    I squint up and
Vertigo
Unbalances the clouds, slithering everything
Into a sack.
                        But a dark horse – a sudden
Little elf-horse – is escaping,

Gallops out of the river
Flashes white chevrons, climbs

The avalanche of leaves, flickering pennons,
Whinnies overhead –

And is snatched
Twisting
Away up

The drumming chimney.

The Weasels We Smoked out of the Bank

Ran along the rowan branch, a whole family,
Furious with ill-contained lightning
Over the ferny falls of clattering coolant.

After the time-long Creation
Of this hill-sculpture, this prone, horizon-long
Limb-jumble of near-female

The wild gentle god of everywhereness
Worships her, in a lark-rapture silence.

But the demons who did all the labouring
Run in and out of her holes

Crackling with redundant energy.

While She Chews Sideways

He gently noses the high point of her rear-end
Then lower and on each side of the tail,
Then flattens one ear, and gazes away, then decidedly
    turns, wheels,
And moves in on the pink-eyed long-horned grey.
He sniffs the length of her spine, arching slightly
And shitting a tumble-thud shit as he does so.
Now he's testy.
He takes a push at the crazy Galloway with the laid-back
    ears.
Now strolling away from them all, his aim at the corner
    gate.
He is scratching himself on the fence, his vibration
Travels the length of the wire.
His barrel bulk is a bit ugly.
As bulls go he's no beauty.
His balls swing in their sock, one side idle.
His skin is utility white, shit-patched,
Pink sinewed at the groin, and the dewlap nearly naked.
A feathery long permed bush of silky white tail –
It hangs straight like a bell rope
From the power-strake of his spine.
He eats steadily, not a cow in the field is open,
His gristly pinkish head, like a shaved blood-hound,
Jerking at the grass.
Overmuch muscle on the thighs, jerk-weight settling
Of each foot, as he eats forward.
His dangle tassel swings, his whole mind
Anchored to it and now dormant.
He's feeding disgustedly, impatiently, carelessly.
His nudity is a bit disgusting. Overmuscled

And a bit shameful, like an overdeveloped body-builder.
He has a juvenile look, a delinquent eye
Very unlikable as he lifts his nostrils
And his upper lip, to test a newcomer.
Today none of that mooning around after cows,
That trundling obedience, like a trailer. None of the cows
Have any power today, and he's stopped looking.
He lays his head sideways, and worries the grass,
Keeping his intake steady.

Magpie

The licensed clown – chak chak!
With no proper part in the play –
Puts his remark in each scene.

Standing on presage, in duplicate, in triplicate,
A laundered puffball,
A sky-skiff, with his one oar.

At every picture's edge, on the top twig,
He watches. He dozes. Working for Fate.
Quick-eyed Mercury, the go-between –

A rattling laugh at the world's blind weight,
A pilfering gleam on its oversights –
These are his perks.

In his whites, his innocence of colour,
In his blacks, infra and ultra,
He struts across the tragic rainbow.

Between caterpillar and diamond.

The Bear

for Alan Hancox

The day darkened in rain. In the bottom of the gorge
The big tarp awning we sat approximately under
Bucked in its ropes. Pans took off.
Nothing we could do
Could alter anything. River rising by the minute.
The rapids churning fog. Ron came in:
'The rain's warm! Feel the warmth of that wind!'

The mountains stood above us in their saunas.
Our flood-indicators were the cataracts
Dangling down their chests and faces
From under their hoods of snow.

When would the rain end?
Maybe it wouldn't, maybe this was The Rains –
The winter coming early. Maybe the river
Never would surrender Ehor's wine-cache
Already four feet under the sliding concrete
Till maybe next June. So why were we happy?
How could we get out? We couldn't.
What else could we be doing? Nothing.
Hands tight hidden, hats down over our ears.
Patience welled up like a comfort.
And Life, said Jay, is simple – just a clock
Of good cooking and even better coffee.
And of calculating, shouted Ehor,
By those heavenly egg-timers above us
Occasionally to be glimpsed through the cloud-rags,
And by the deepening bow-wave of that log-jam
What a fantastic upriver flood of Steelhead

This will leave us to deal with!
This gloomy wash-out, my friends, is our bonanza!
And the streamy danglers
That decorate the mountains' Indian faces
Mean the rain is getting excited for us
And wanting the mountains to dance. It has dressed the
    mountains
For a dance – the dance of the Steelhead,
The snow-melt rain-storm dance. And those ribbons
Are our dance regalia –

We could have appreciated it all,
We could have let the spirits, clamped in our
    weatherproofs,
Magnify themselves and dance with the mountains
And the whirling wind in robes
Of rain and elemental nostalgia –
But what those busy tickertapes were telling
Was bigger water, river out of control,
The Steelhead hugging deeper
As if they were under an avalanche
Their more and more unthinkable finger-holds,
While our fishing days and our flown-in dreams
Rumbled away over them tossing driftwood,
Bleeding us downstream. Our dance was to sit tight,
Freshly sawn-off stumps, hugging our roots,
Stumps of abandoned sawn-off totem poles
At a glum remove from our enterprise
Suspended in the clouds literally,
Clouds that were dragging up and down the gorge
Simultaneously in opposite directions,
A dance that mimed the hope of hopelessness
To squalls that slapped gunshots out of the tent,

Our gossip out of our mouths, and scattered our coffee.

While rain ripped at the tarp. And taps were spluttering
At every corner – every edge tasselled or bucketing
As the tarp jumped. And dangledrops were descending
Along every cord, or snapped off.
We could only watch it all and know
Everything was worsening.
                                                    But we sat there
And enjoyed it. And the Steelhead down there
They were enjoying it too, this was what they were made
    of,
And made by, and made for, this was their moment.
The thousand-mile humping of mountains
That looked immovable, was in a frenzy,
Melt of snows metabolism of stars,
Was shivering to its ecstasy in the Steelhead.
This actually was the love-act that had brought them
Out of everywhere, squirming and leaping,
And that had brought us too – besotted voyeurs –
Trying to hook ourselves into it.
And all the giddy orgasm of the river
Quaking under our feet –

                                        'What's that? It's a bear!'
A black snag reeled past on the blue-white swirls – a tree
    root?
'It's a goddamned bear!' It was a bear.
The night before's mystery upstream gunshot
Materialized, saluted us, and vanished
As a black sea-going bear, a scapegoat, an offering.

Pheasant

Rama, in a horned blood-mask,
As a reptile of bronze leaves,
Steps from a shivering furnace.

Already the whole cloak of landscape
With flame-soft clashings
Trails after his fashion.

In the sun's open door,
On a leafless black branch,
The Pheasant
Ruffles his burning book.

Darkens into a deep tapestry
Hung from Orion
Where the Dog's tongue smokes twilight
And gun barrels blue brittle as frost.

With his inlaid head in the East
The pheasant cools
Among the day's embers
On the finger of Lord Buddha – in Great Peace

Where the fox's icicles
Melt into moon,
And the poachers' sulphur
Suffers only in an opposite mirror –

Upside down, with gape in a bag of blood,
Among goblin pigs' ears
At a disembowelled trance-dancing
Of hare-priests.

The Bull Moses

A hoist up and I could lean over
The upper edge of the high half-door,
My left foot ledged on the hinge, and look in at the
   byre's
Blaze of darkness: a sudden shut-eyed look
Backward into the head.
                         Blackness is depth
Beyond star. But the warm weight of his breathing,
The ammoniac reek of his litter, the hotly-tongued
Mash of his cud, steamed against me.
Then, slowly, as onto the mind's eye –
The brow like masonry, the deep-keeled neck:
Something come up there onto the brink of the gulf,
Hadn't heard of the world, too deep in itself to be called
   to,
Stood in sleep. He would swing his muzzle at a fly
But the square of sky where I hung, shouting, waving,
Was nothing to him; nothing of our light
Found any reflection in him.
                         Each dusk the farmer led
   him
Down to the pond to drink and smell the air,
And he took no pace but the farmer
Led him to take it, as if he knew nothing
Of the ages and continents of his fathers,
Shut, while he wombed, to a dark shed
And steps between his door and the duck pond;
The weight of the sun and the moon and the world
   hammered
To a ring of brass through his nostrils.
                         He would raise

His streaming muzzle and look out over the meadows,
But the grasses whispered nothing awake, the fetch
Of the distance drew nothing to momentum
In the locked black of his powers. He came strolling gently
    back,
Paused neither toward the pig-pens on his right,
Nor toward the cow-byres on his left: something
Deliberate in his leisure, some beheld future
Founding in his quiet.

                 I kept the door wide,
Closed it after him and pushed the bolt.

Performance

Just before the curtain falls in the river
The Damselfly, with offstage, inaudible shriek
Reappears, weightless.

Hover-poised, in her snake-skin leotards,
Her violet-dark elegance.

Eyelash-delicate, a dracula beauty,
In her acetylene jewels.

Her mascara smudged, her veils shimmer-fresh –

Late August. Some sycamore leaves
Already in their museum, eaten to lace.
Robin song bronze-touching the stillness
Over posthumous nettles. The swifts, as one,
Whipcracked, gone. Blackberries.
                                    And now, lightly,
Adder-shock of this dainty assassin
Still in mid-passion –
                        still in her miracle play:
Masked, archaic, mute, insect mystery
Out of the sun's crypt.
                        Everything is forgiven
Such a metamorphosis in love!
Phaedra Titania
Dragon of crazed enamels!
Tragedienne of the ultra-violet,
So sulphurous and so frail,

Stepping so magnetically to her doom!

Lifted out of the river with tweezers
Dripping the sun's incandescence –

                              suddenly she
Switches her scene elsewhere.

      (Find him later, halfway up a nettle,
      A touch-crumple petal of web and dew –

      Midget puppet-clown, tranced on his strings,
      In the nightfall pall of balsam.)

Irish Elk

Here stood the Irish Elk
In its castle of gristle
Its machinery of pain
Staring around, under its absurd furniture.

It browsed a little, it shivered,
Then clattered to some other draughty standing place,
Improbably balanced
On the sea of skylines.

The geography was amended.
The Elk's ceremony became redundant.
That eye accepted the verdict
Like a hero, without change of expression.

The mystery of Elk was unravelled.

The waters of Elk have gone.

The bog-cotton drank them.

Now let the memorial of Elk
Be the harebell

Feeding upwind.

September Salmon

Famously home from sea,
Nobly preoccupied with his marriage licence,
He ignores the weir's wrangle. Ignores
The parochial down-drag
Of the pool's long diphthong. Ignores
Festivals of insect fluorescence.

He serves his descendants. And his homage
Is to be patient, performing, slowly, the palsy
Of concerted autumn
In the upside-down cage of a tree.

Does he envy the perennial eels and the mongrel
     minnows?
He is becoming a god,
A tree of sexual death, sacred with lichens.

Sometimes, for days, lost to himself.
                              Mid-morning,
At the right angle of sun
You can see the floor of his chapel.
There he sways at the altar –
A soul
Hovering in the incantation and the incense.

Over his sky the skeeters traffic, godlike and double-
     jointed.
He lifts
To the molten palette of the mercurial light
And adds his daub.

A Rival

The cormorant, commissar of the hard sea,
Has not adjusted to the soft river.

He lifts his pterodactyl head in the drought pool
(Sound-proof cellar of final solutions).

The dinosaur massacre-machine
Hums on in his skull, programme unaltered.

That fossil eye-chip could reduce
All the blood in the world, yet still taste nothing.

At dawn he's at it, under the sick face –
Cancer in the lymph, uncontrollable.

Level your eye's aim and he's off
Knocking things over, out through the window –

An abortion-doctor
Black bag packed with vital organs

Dripping unspeakably.
                            Then away, heavy, high
Over the sea's iron curtain –

The pool lies there mutilated,
                            face averted,
Dumb and ruined.

Very New Foal

        The moorland mother's
Dirty white. Perfunctory
She goes on shortening the short grass,
Leaning onto her nibble, at the road's edge
With a few other new mothers. Sun
Comes down warm, through the hard wind
That goes over the ridge.
        The new foal
Is dirtier than his mother. Maybe
He'll grow to be a dappled grey. Maybe not.
At the moment he's not much of anything.
He's up and spellbound, hanging his head
Which is still womb-rounded, primeval
Lizard shoe-shaped, not noble bony
Or stress-delicate horse-like, or alert
Lifted into the trembling fringe of senses,
But sleepy, terribly sleepy, eyes
Just glad to sink back dozy, head
Hanging in mother-comfort, fringed with sun-glow,
The dainty curl of beard in sun-glow,
Drying out, and the knotty plait of mane
Drying out, and the knotty, twisty
Plait of tail drying to looseness. He leans
Onto his shoulders, stretching
His embryo curve straight, reflexing
The new soft bow of his spine,
And his hind-knees lean together,
Taking a rest one against the other
Even as he stretches. He positions
His front legs, discovering
How tables stay steady. He dozes

There in mid-stretch, slackening,
His head hanging, tired with surprise,
His nose hanging out there, heavy,
In front of his eyes.
                    Others
Not much older, only hours older,
Sit like little horses, near mothers,
Legs cleverly folded already
Tightly compact, keeping the world out,
But their necks up, and arched
Like the necks of sea-horses, and their heads
Bowed at just that angle. Just the angle,
Half-sleep and half-pride, of swans
Shouldering their splendour along,
Breasting the world-surge, hanging in sleep,
Slightly tucked-in chins, like sea-horses,
Such a sleepy, poised angle. A pose
Brought from the other world, a deeper place
Where Seraphim surge in sleep-stillness,
Breasting waves of light, their eyes
Lowered, their brows
Fronting the source, the bulging towards them
Of the world, the world's hum, the small cries.

A Macaw

Sorcerer! How you hate it all!
Trampling it under slowly – kneading it all
To an ectoplasmic pulp.

Your trampling is your dance. With your eye –
Your head-writhing
Evil eye – fixing the enemy,

You writhe you weave you entangle
All the cords of his soul
And so drag him towards you, and trample him under.

Gomorrah! Sodom! Your eye squirms on its pin
In its socket of ashes. In the sulphurous hand-axe
You have to use for a face. That cowl,

That visor of black flint,
Is also your third foot. And your flint cup
Serves you for under-jaw, crudely chipped to fit.

Such a pale eye will never forgive!
The egg-daub daffodil shirt
Is no consolation. And that puppet

Prussian-blue hauberk of feathers
Is a mockery.
                    Nothing will help, you know,
When you come, finally, to grips

With the dancing stars
Who devised this
Trembling degradation and prison and this

Torture instrument of brittle plastic
Jammed askew
Athwart your gullet.

Whiteness

Walks the river at dawn.

The thorn-tree hiding its thorns
With too much and too fleshy perfume.

Thin water. Uneasy ghost.
Whorls clotted with petals.

Trout, like a hidden man's cough,
Slash under dripping roots.

Heron. Clang
Coiling its snake in heavy hurry
Hoists away, yanked away

Ceases to ponder the cuneiform
Under glass

Huge owl-lump of dawn
With wrong fittings, a parasol broken
Tumbles up into strong sky

Banks precariously, risks a look
A writhing unmade bedstead

Sets the blade between its shoulders
And hang-falls
Down a long aim

Dangles its reeds

Till it can see its own pale eyes
Suddenly shakes off cumbersome cloud
To anchor, tall,
An open question.

Now only the river nags to be elsewhere.

Curlews

I

They lift
Out of the maternal watery blue lines

Stripped of all but their cry
Some twists of near-inedible sinew

They slough off
The robes of bilberry blue
The cloud-stained bogland

They veer up and eddy away over
The stone horns

They trail a long, dangling, falling aim
Across water

Lancing their voices
Through the skin of this light

Drinking the nameless and naked
Through trembling bills.

II

Curlews in April
Hang their harps over the misty valleys

A wobbling water-call
A wet-footed god of the horizons

New moons sink into the heather
And full golden moons

Bulge over spent walls.

Couples under Cover

The ewes are in the shed
Under clapping wings of corrugated iron
Where entering rays of snow cut horizontal
Fiery and radioactive, a star dust.
The oaks outside, half digested
With a writhing white fire-snow off the hill-field
Burning to frails of charcoal,
Roar blind, and swing blindly, a hilltop
Helpless self-defence. Snow
Is erasing them, whitening blanks
Against a dirty whiteness. The new jolly lambs
Are pleased with their nursery. A few cavorts
Keep trying their hind legs – up and a twist,
So they stagger back to balance, bewildered
By the life that's working at them. Heads, safer,
Home in on udders, undergroin hot flesh tent,
Hide eyes in muggy snugness. The ewes can't settle,
Heads bony and ratty with anxiety,
Keyed to every wind shift, light-footed
To leap clear when the hilltop
Starts to peel off, or those tortured tree-oceans
Come blundering through the old stonework.
They don't appreciate the comfort.
They'd as soon be in midfield suffering
The twenty-mile snow gale of unprotection,
Ice balls anaesthetizing their back-end blood tatters,
Watching and worrying while a lamb grows stranger –
A rumpy-humped skinned-looking rabbit
Whose hunger no longer works.
                                One day
Of slightly unnatural comfort, and the lambs

Will toss out into the snow, imperishable,
Like trawlers, bobbing in gangs, while the world
Welters unconscious into whiteness.

Starlings Have Come

A horde out of sub-Arctic Asia
Darkening nightfall, a faint sky-roar
Of pressure on the ear.

More thicken the vortex, gloomier.

A bacteria cyclone, a writhing of imps
Issuing from a hole in the horizon
Topples and blackens a whole farm.

Now a close-up seething of fleas.
                              And now a silence –
The doom-panic mob listens, for a second.
Then, with a soft boom, they wrap you
Into their mind-warp, assembling a nightmare sky-wheel
Of escape – a Niagara
Of upward rumbling wings – that collapses again

In an unmanageable weight
Of neurotic atoms.
                    They're the subconscious
Of the Smart-Alec, all slick hair and Adam's apple,
Sunday chimney starling.
                          This Elizabethan songster,
Italianate, in damask, emblematic,
Trembles his ruff, pierces the Maytime
With his perfected whistle
Of a falling bomb – or frenzies himself
Into a Gothic, dishevelled madness,
Chattering his skeleton, sucking his brains,
Gargling his blood through a tin flute –
                              Ah, Shepster!
Suddenly such a bare dagger of listening!

Next thing – down at the bread
Screeching like a cat
Limber and saurian on your hind legs,

Tumbling the sparrows with a drop kick –

A Satanic hoodlum, a cross-eyed boss,
Black body crammed with hot rubies
And Anthrax under your nails.

A Cranefly in September

She is struggling through grass-mesh – not flying,
Her wide-winged, stiff, weightless basket-work of limbs
Rocking, like an antique wain, a top-heavy ceremonial
    cart
Across mountain summits
(Not planing over water, dipping her tail)
But blundering with long strides, long reachings, reelings
And ginger-glistening wings
From collison to collision.
Aimless in no particular direction,
Just exerting her last to escape out of the overwhelming
Of whatever it is, legs, grass,
The garden, the county, the country, the world –

Sometimes she rests long minutes in the grass forest
Like a fairytale hero, only a marvel can help her.
She cannot fathom the mystery of this forest
In which, for instance, this giant watches –
The giant who knows she cannot be helped in any way.

Her jointed bamboo fuselage,
Her lobster shoulders, and her face
Like a pinhead dragon, with its tender moustache,
And the simple colourless church windows of her wings
Will come to an end, in mid-search, quite soon.
Everything about her, every perfected vestment
Is already superfluous.
The monstrous excess of her legs and curly feet
Are a problem beyond her.
The calculus of glucose and chitin inadequate
To plot her through the infinities of the stems.

The frayed apple leaves, the grunting raven, the defunct
  tractor
Sunk in nettles, wait with their multiplications
Like other galaxies.
The sky's northward September procession, the vast soft
  armistice,
Like an empire on the move,
Abandons her, tinily embattled
With her cumbering limbs and cumbered brain.

Birth of Rainbow

This morning blue vast clarity of March sky
But a blustery violence of air, and a soaked overnight
New-painted look to the world. The wind coming
Off the snowed moor in the south, razorish,
Heavy-bladed and head-cutting, off snow-powdered
   ridges.
Flooded ruts shook. Hoof puddles flashed. A daisy
Mud-plastered unmixed its head from the mud.
The black and white cow, on the highest crest of the round
   ridge,
Stood under the end of a rainbow,
Head down licking something, full in the painful wind
That the pouring haze of the rainbow ignored.
She was licking her gawky black calf
Collapsed wet-fresh from the womb, blinking his eyes
In the low morning dazzling washed sun.
Black, wet as a collie from a river, as she licked him,
Finding his smells, learning his particularity.
A flag of bloody tissue hung from her back end –
Spreading and shining, pink-fleshed and raw, it flapped and
   coiled
In the unsparing wind. She positioned herself, uneasy
As we approached, nervous small footwork
On the hoof-ploughed drowned sod of the ruined field.
She made uneasy low noises, and her calf too
With his staring whites, mooed the full clear calf-note
Pure as woodwind, and tried to get up,
Tried to get his cantilever front legs
In operation, lifted his shoulders, hoisted to his knees,
Then hoisted his back end and lurched forward
On his knees and crumpling ankles, sliding in the mud

And collapsing plastered. She went on licking him.
She started eating the banner of thin raw flesh that
Spinnakered from her rear. We left her to it.
Blobbed antiseptic onto the sodden blood-dangle
Of his muddy birth cord, and left her
Inspecting the new smell. The whole South West
Was black as nightfall.
Trailing squall-smokes hung over the moor, leaning
And whitening toward us, then the world blurred
And disappeared in forty-five-degree hail
And a gate-jerking blast. We got to cover.
Left to God the calf and his mother.

Tern

for Norman Nicholson

The breaker humps its green glass.
You see the sunrise through it, the wrack dark in it,
And over it – the bird of sickles
Swimming in the wind, with oiled spasm.

That is the tern. A blood-tipped harpoon
Hollow-ground in the roller-dazzle,
Honed in the wind-flash, polished
By his own expertise –

Now finished and in use.
The wings – remote-controlled
By the eyes
In his submarine swift shadow

Feint and tilt in their steel.
Suddenly a triggered magnet
Connects him downward, through a thin shatter,
To a sand-eel. He hoists out, with a twinkling,

Through some other wave-window.
His eye is a gimlet.
Deep in the churned grain of the roller
His brain is a gimlet. He hangs,

A blown tatter, a precarious word
In the mouth of ocean pronouncements.
His meaning has no margin. He shudders
To the tips of his tail-tines.

Momentarily, his lit scrap is a shriek.

Buzz in the Window

                                        Buzz frantic
And prolonged. Fly down near the corner,
The cemetery den. A big blue-fly
Is trying to drag a plough, too deep
In earth too stony, immovable. Then the fly
Buzzing its full revs forward, budges backward.
Clings. Deadlock.
The spider has gripped its anus. Slender talons
Test the blue armour gently, the head
Buried in the big game. He tugs
Tigerish, half the size of his prey. A pounding
Glory-time for the spider. For the other
A darkening summary of some circumstances
In the window-corner, with a dead bee,
Wing-petals, husks of insect-armour, a brambled
Glade of dusty web. It buzzes less
As the drug argues deeper and deeper.
In fluttery soundless tremors it tries to keep
A hold on the air. The north sky
Moves northward. The blossom is clinging
To its hopes, refurnishing the constant
Of ignorant life. The blue-fly,
Without changing expression, only adjusting
Its leg-stance, as if to more comfort,
Undergoes ultimate ghastliness. Finally agrees to it.
The spider tugs, retreating. The fly
Is going to let it do everything. Something is stuck.
The fly is fouled in web. Intelligence, the spider,
Comes round to look and patiently, joyfully,
Starts cutting the mesh. Frees it. Returns

To the haul – homeward in that exhausted ecstasy
The loaded hunters of the Pleistocene
Never recorded either.

The Kingfisher

The Kingfisher perches. He studies.

Escaped from the jeweller's opium
X-rays the river's toppling
Tangle of glooms.

Now he's vanished – into vibrations.
A sudden electric wire, jarred rigid,
Snaps – with a blue flare.

He has left his needle buried in your ear.

Oafish oaks, kneeling, bend over
Dragging with their reflections
For the sunken stones. The Kingfisher
Erupts through the mirror, beak full of ingots,

And is away – cutting the one straight line
Of the raggle-taggle tumbledown river
With a diamond –

Leaves a rainbow splinter sticking in your eye.

Through him, God, whizzing in the sun,
Glimpses the angler.

Through him, God
Marries a pit
Of fishy mire.
                And look! He's
– gone again.
                Spark, sapphire, refracted
From beyond water
Shivering the spine of the river.

An Eel

The strange part is his head. Her head. The strangely
   ripened
Domes over the brain, swollen nacelles
For some large containment. Lobed glands
Of some large awareness. Eerie the eel's head.
This full, plum-sleeked fruit of evolution.
Beneath it, her snout's a squashed slipper-face,
The mouth grin-long and perfunctory,
Undershot predatory. And the iris, dirty gold
Distilled only enough to be different
From the olive lode of her body,
The grained and woven blacks. And ringed larger
With a vaguer vision, an earlier eye
Behind her eye, paler, blinder,
Inward. Her buffalo hump
Begins the amazement of her progress.
Her mid-shoulder pectoral fin – concession
To fish-life – secretes itself
Flush with her concealing suit: under it
The skin's a pale exposure of deepest eel
As her belly is, a dulled pearl.
Strangest, the thumb-print skin, the rubberized weave
Of her insulation. Her whole body
Damascened with identity. This is she
Suspends the Sargasso
In her inmost hope. Her life is a cell
Sealed from event, her patience
Global and furthered with love
By the bending stars as if she

Were earth's sole initiate. Alone
In her millions, the moon's pilgrim,
The nun of water.

II

Where does the river come from?
And the eel, the night-mind of water –
The river within the river and opposite –
The night-nerve of water?

Not from the earth's remembering mire
Not from the air's whim
Not from the brimming sun. Where from?

From the bottom of the nothing pool
Sargasso of God
Out of the empty spiral of stars

A glimmering person.

The Mayfly is Frail

The way the shivering Northern Lights are frail.

Erupting floods, flood-lava drag across farms,
Oak-roots cartwheeling –
The inspiration was seismic.

Some mad sculptor
In frenzy remaking the river's rooms
Through days and nights of bulging shoulders
And dull bellowing – cooled with cloudbursts –
Needed all his temperament.

Now he sprawls – flat in the sun –
Apparently burned out.

And now comes the still small voice.

Out of his glowing exhaustion
Heals a giddy mote,
A purity in a mould

And the mould splits at a touch of the air.

A shimmering beast
Dawns from the river's opened side.

A Mountain Lion

　　　　　　Her alarmed skulk
Fearing to peel her molten umber
From shadows –
　　　　　　Her forefeet
Go forward daringly, a venture, a theft in them
Stealing her body away after –

She weaves, her banner's soft prisoner,
In her element of silence, weaving silence
Like a dance, a living silence
Making herself invisible magical steps
Weaving a silence into all her limbs

She flows along, just inside the air
Every line eluding the eye. Hesitation
And moving beyond
And by hesitation. All her legs like
A magical multiplication of one leg
Look at any one, the others are doing the walking
And plank-slender and pressing
Forward through silence, becoming silence
Ahead and leaving it behind, travelling
Like a sound-wave, arriving suddenly.
Ahead of herself, a swift stillness.

Two Tortoiseshell Butterflies

Mid-May – after May frosts that killed the Camellias,
After May snow. After a winter
Worst in human memory, a freeze
Killing the hundred year old Bay Tree,
And the ten year old Bay Tree – suddenly
A warm limpness. A blue heaven just veiled
With the sweatings of earth
And with the sweatings-out of winter
Feverish under the piled
Maywear of the lawn.
                                    Now two
Tortoiseshell butterflies, finding themselves alive,
She drunk with the earth-sweat, and he
Drunk with her, float in eddies
Over the Daisies' quilt. She prefers Dandelions,
Settling to nod her long spring tongue down
Into the nestling pleats, into the flower's
Thick-folded throat, her wings high-folded.
He settling behind her, among plain glistenings
Of the new grass, edging and twitching
To nearly touch – pulsing and convulsing
Wings wide open to tight-closed to flat open
Quivering to keep her so near, almost reaching
To stroke her abdomen with his antennae –
Then she's up and away, and he startlingly
Swallowlike overtaking, crowding her, heading her
Off any escape. She turns that
To her purpose, and veers down
Onto another Dandelion, attaching
Her weightless yacht to its crest.
Wobbles to stronger hold, to deeper, sweeter

Penetration, her wings tight shut above her,
A sealed book, absorbed in itself.
She ignores him
Where he edges to left and to right, flitting
His wings open, titillating her fur
With his perfumed draughts, spasming his patterns,
His tropical, pheasant appeals of folk art,
Venturing closer, grass-blade by grass-blade,
Trembling with inhibition, nearly touching –
And again she's away, dithering blackly. He swoops
On an elastic to settle accurately
Under her tail again as she clamps to
This time a Daisy. She's been chosen,
Courtship has claimed her. And he's been conscripted
To what's required
Of the splitting bud, of the talented robin
That performs piercings
Out of the still-bare ash,
The whole air just like him, just breathing
Over the still-turned-inward earth, the first
Caresses of the wedding coming, the earth
Opening its petals, the whole sky
Opening a flower
Of unfathomably-patterned pollen.

A Cormorant

Here before me, snake-head.
My waders weigh seven pounds.

My Barbour jacket, mainly necessary
For its pockets, is proof

Against the sky at my back. My bag
Sags with lures and hunter's medicine enough

For a year in the Palaeolithic.
My hat, of use only

If this May relapses to March
Embarrasses me, and my net, long as myself,

Optimistic, awkward, infatuated
With every twig-snag and fence-barb

Will slowly ruin the day. I paddle
Precariously on slimed shale,

And infiltrate twenty yards
Of gluey and magnetized spider-gleam

Into the elbowing dense jostle-traffic
Of the river's tunnel, and pray

With futuristic, archaic under-breath
So that some fish, telepathically overpowered,

Will attach its incomprehension
To the bauble I offer to space in general.

The cormorant eyes me, beak uptilted,
Body-snake low – sea-serpentish.

He's thinking: 'There's one of those monsters.
Dare I risk another dive?' He dives.

He sheds everything from his tail-end
Except fish-action, becomes fish,

Disappears from bird,
Dissolving himself

Into fish, so dissolving fish naturally
Into himself. Re-emerges, gorged,

Himself as he was, and escapes me,
Leaves me high and dry in my space-armour,

A deep-sea diver in two inches of water.

Nightjar

The tree creeps on its knees.
The dead branch aims, in the last light.
The cat bird is telescopic.

The sun's escape
Shudders shot
By wings of ashes.

The moon falls, with all its moths,
Into a bird's face.

Stars spark
From the rasp of its cry.

Till the moon-eater, cooling,
Yawns dawn
And sleeps bark.

Manchester Skytrain

Remember that nightmare straight into the camera –
Dice among dice, jounced in a jouncing cup.
Never any nearer, bouncing in a huddle, on the spot.
Struggling all together glued in a clot.

The first dead cert I ever backed was Word
From The Owner's Mouth. Week before
There was my jockey – 'a day in the life of' –
Starred in *Picture Post*. Who? Somewhere

In the nineteen forty-seven
Strata of the British Museum.
He's gone. He went
Even as I watched. And the horse's name?

Gone with my money. It cartwheeled
Smack in front of me, over the first fence.
Left its jockey flat – killed – and galloped on
Long after the finish, in a drugged trance –

(Doncaster). One can't bear to be groomed:
Arcs into shudders, chewing at a scream.
One rolls on the ground and whirls hammers
Refusing to cross a stream,

Ending up shot. The stables – asylums
Of these blue-blooded insane –
Prefer the introverts. Here's one. A razor-faced
Big-eyed schizophrene.

Every known musical instrument,
The whole ensemble, packed
Into a top-heavy, twangling half ton
On the stilts of an insect.

They're all dangerous to touch. It nearly takes off –
Just stays. Like a flying saucer's
Anti-gravity coil magnet, still space-radioactive,
Eased hot from the wreck. It scares

Even itself. We stand, nervous. Metaphors
Fail the field of force.
Jokey disparagements
The torque of vertigo. A dark horse.

February 17th

A lamb could not get born. Ice wind
Out of a downpour dishclout sunrise. The mother
Lay on the mudded slope. Harried, she got up
And the blackish lump bobbed at her back end
Under her tail. After some hard galloping,
Some manoeuvring, much flapping of the backward
Lump head of the lamb looking out,
I caught her with a rope. Laid her, head uphill,
And examined the lamb. A blood ball swollen
Tight in its black felt, its mouth gap
Squashed crooked, tongue stuck out, black-purple,
Strangled by its mother. I felt inside,
Past the noose of mother-flesh, into the slippery
Muscled tunnel, fingering for a hoof,
Right back to the porthole of the pelvis.
But there was no hoof. He had stuck his head out too
    early
And his feet could not follow. He should have
Felt his way, tiptoe, his toes
Tucked up under his nose
For a safe landing. So I kneeled wrestling
With her groans. No hand could squeeze past
The lamb's neck into her interior
To hook a knee. I roped that baby head
And hauled till she cried out and tried
To get up and I saw it was useless. I went
Two miles for the injection and a razor.
Sliced the lamb's throat-strings, levered with a knife
Between the vertebrae and brought the head off
To stare at its mother, its pipes sitting in the mud
With all earth for a body. Then pushed

The neck stump right back in, and as I pushed
She pushed. She pushed crying and I pushed gasping.
And the strength
Of the birth push and the push of my thumb
Against that wobbly vertebra were deadlock,
A to-fro futility. Till I forced
A hand past and got a knee. Then like
Pulling myself to the ceiling with one finger
Hooked in a loop, timing my effort
To her birth-push groans, I pulled against
The corpse that would not come. Till it came.
And after it the long, sudden, yolk-yellow
Parcel of life
In a smoking slither of oils and soups and syrups –
And the body lay born, beside the hacked-off head.

Evening Thrush

Beyond a twilight of limes and willows
A church craftsman is still busy –
Switing idols,
Rough pre-Goidelic gods and goddesses,
Out of old bits of churchyard yew.

Suddenly flinging
Everything off, head-up, flame-naked
Plunges shuddering into the creator –

Then comes plodding back, with a limp, over cobbles.

That was a virtuoso's joke.

Now, serious, stretched full height, he aims
At the zenith. He situates a note
Right on the source of light.

Sews a seamless garment, simultaneously
Hurls javelins of dew
Three in air together, catches them.

Explains a studied theorem of sober practicality.

Cool-eyed,
Gossips in a mundane code of splutters
With Venus and Jupiter.
                                        Listens –
Motionless, intent astronomer.

Suddenly launches a soul –

The first roses hang in a yolk stupor.
Globe after globe rolls out
Through his fluteful of dew –

The tree-stacks ride out on the widening arc.

Alone and darkening
At the altar of a star
With his sword through his throat
The thrush of clay goes on arguing
Over the graves.

O thrush,
If that really is you, behind the leaf-screen,
Who is this –

Worn-headed, on the lawn's grass, after sunset,
Humped, voiceless, turdus, imprisoned
As a long-distance lorry-driver, dazed

With the pop and static and unending
Of worms and wife and kids?

Coming down through Somerset

I flash-glimpsed in the headlights – the high moment
Of driving through England – a killed badger
Sprawled with helpless legs. Yet again
Manoeuvred lane ends, retracked, waited
Out of decency for headlights to die,
Lifted by one warm hind leg in the world-night
A slain badger. August dust-heat. Beautiful,
Beautiful, warm, secret beast. Bedded him
Passenger, bleeding from the nose. Brought him close
Into my life. Now he lies on the beam
Torn from a great building. Beam waiting two years
To be built into new building. Summer coat
Not worth skinning off him. His skeleton – for the
   future.
Fangs, handsome concealed. Flies, drumming,
Bejewel his transit. Heatwave ushers him hourly
Toward his underworlds. A grim day of flies
And sunbathing. Get rid of that badger.
A night of shrunk rivers, glowing pastures,
Sea-trout shouldering up through trickles. Then the sun
   again
Waking like a torn-out eye. How strangely
He stays on into the dawn – how quiet
The dark bear-claws, the long frost-tipped guard hairs!
Get rid of that badger today.
And already the flies
More passionate, bringing their friends. I don't want
To bury and waste him. Or skin him (it is too late).
Or hack off his head and boil it
To liberate his masterpiece skull. I want him
To stay as he is. Sooty gloss-throated,

With his perfect face. Paws so tired,
Power-body relegated. I want him
To stop time. His strength staying, bulky,
Blocking time. His rankness, his bristling wildness,
His thrillingly painted face.
A badger on my moment of life.
Not years ago, like the others, but now.
I stand
Watching his stillness, like an iron nail
Driven, flush to the head,
Into a yew post. Something has to stay.

Tiger

At the junction of beauty and danger
The tiger's scroll becomes legible.
In relief, he moves through an impotent chaos.
The Creator is his nearest neighbour.
The mild, frosty, majestic mandala
Of his face, to spirit hospitable
As to flesh. With easy latitude
He composes his mass.
He exhales benediction,
Malediction. Privileged
At the paradoxical cross-junction
Of good and evil, and beyond both.
His own ego is unobtrusive
Among the jungle babblers,
His engineering faultlessly secure.
In a fate like an allegory
Of God-all-but-forgotten, he balances modestly
The bloodmarks of his canvas
And the long-grass dawn beauty
As the engraved moment of lightning
On the doomsday skin of the Universe.

Roe Deer

In the dawn-dirty light, in the biggest snow of the year
Two blue-dark deer stood in the road, alerted.

They had happened into my dimension
The moment I was arriving just there.

They planted their two or three years of secret deerhood
Clear on my snow-screen vision of the abnormal

And hesitated in the all-way disintegration
And stared at me. And so for some lasting seconds

I could think the deer were waiting for me
To remember the password and sign

That the curtain had blown aside for a moment
And there where the trees were no longer trees, nor the road
   a road

The deer had come for me.

Then they ducked through the hedge, and upright they
   rode their legs
Away downhill over a snow-lonely field

Towards tree-dark – finally
Seeming to eddy and glide and fly away up

Into the boil of big flakes.
The snow took them and soon their nearby hoofprints as
   well

Revising its dawn inspiration
Back to the ordinary.

Bullfrog

With their lithe long strong legs
Some frogs are able
To thump upon double-
Bass strings though pond-water deadens and clogs.

But you, bullfrog, you pump out
Whole fogs full of horn – a threat
As of a liner looming. True
That, first hearing you
Disgorging your gouts of darkness like a wounded god,
Not utterly fantastical I expected
(As in some antique tale depicted)
A broken-down bull up to its belly in mud,
Sucking black swamp up, belching out black cloud

And a squall of gudgeon and lilies.
                              A surprise,
To see you, a boy's prize,
No bigger than a rat – all dumb silence
In your little old woman hands.

Crow and the Birds

When the eagle soared clear through a dawn distilling of
emerald
When the curlew trawled in seadusk through a chime of
wineglasses
When the swallow swooped through a woman's song in
a cavern
And the swift flicked through the breath of a violet

When the owl sailed clear of tomorrow's conscience
And the sparrow preened himself of yesterday's promise
And the heron laboured clear of the Bessemer upglare
And the bluetit zipped clear of lace panties
And the woodpecker drummed clear of the rotovator and
the rose-farm
And the peewit tumbled clear of the laundromat

While the bullfinch plumped in the apple bud
And the goldfinch bulbed in the sun
And the wryneck crooked in the moon
And the dipper peered from the dewball

Crow spraddled head-down in the beach-garbage,
guzzling a dropped ice-cream.

Macaw and Little Miss

    In a cage of wire-ribs
The size of a man's head, the macaw bristles in a staring
Combusion, suffers the stoking devils of his eyes.
In the old lady's parlour, where an aspidistra succumbs
To the musk of faded velvet, he hangs as in clear flames,
    Like a torturer's iron instrument preparing
    With dense slow shudderings of greens, yellows, blues,
      Crimsoning into the barbs:

    Or like the smouldering head that hung
In Killdevil's brass kitchen, in irons, who had been
Volcano swearing to vomit the world away in black ash,
And would, one day; or a fugitive aristocrat
From some thunderous mythological hierarchy, caught
    By a little boy with a crust and a bent pin,
    Or snare of horsehair set for a song-thrush,
      And put in a cage to sing.

    The old lady who feeds him seeds
Has a grand-daughter. The girl calls him 'Poor Polly', pokes fun.
'Jolly Mop'. But lies under every full moon,
The spun glass of her body bared and so gleam-still
Her brimming eyes do not tremble or spill
    The dream where the warrior comes, lightning and iron,
    Smashing and burning and rending towards her loin:
      Deep into her pillow her silence pleads.

All day he stares at his furnace
With eyes red-raw, but when she comes they close.
'Polly. Pretty Poll', she cajoles, and rocks him gently.
She caresses, whispers kisses. The blue lids stay shut.
She strikes the cage in a tantrum and swirls out:
    Instantly beak, wings, talons crash
    The bars in conflagration and frenzy,
        And his shriek shakes the house.

Meeting

He smiles in a mirror, shrinking the whole
Sun-swung zodiac of light to a trinket shape
   On the rise of his eye: it is a role

In which he can fling a cape,
And outloom life like Faustus. But once when
   On an empty mountain slope

A black goat clattered and ran
Towards him, and set forefeet firm on a rock
   Above and looked down

A square-pupilled yellow-eyed look,
The black devil head against the blue air,
   What gigantic fingers took

Him up and on a bare
Palm turned him close under an eye
   That was like a living hanging hemisphere

And watched his blood's gleam with a ray
Slow and cold and ferocious as a star
   Till the goat clattered away.

Happy Calf

Mother is worried, her low, short moos
Question what's going on. But her calf
Is quite happy, resting on his elbows,
With his wrists folded under, and his precious hind legs
Brought up beside him, his little hooves
Of hardly-used yellow-soled black.
She looms up, to reassure him with heavy lickings.
He wishes she'd go away. He's meditating
Black as a mole and as velvety,
With a white face-mask, and a pink parting,
With black tear-patches, but long
Glamorous white eyelashes. A mild narrowing
Of his eyes, as he lies, testing each breath
For its peculiar flavour of being alive.
Such a pink muzzle, but a black dap
Where he just touched his mother's blackness
With a tentative sniff. He is all quiet
While his mother worries to and fro, grazes a little,
Then looks back, a shapely mass
Against the south sky and the low frieze of hills,
And moos questioning warning. He just stays,
Head slightly tilted, in the mild illness
Of being quite contented, and patient
With all the busyness inside him, the growing
Getting under way. The wind from the north
Marching the high silvery floor of clouds
Trembles the grass-stalks near him. His head wobbles
Infinitesimally in the pulse of his life.
A buttercup leans on his velvet hip.
He folds his head back little by breathed little
Till it rests on his shoulder, his nose on his ankle,
And he sleeps. Only his ears stay awake.

Sources

The poems in this book were first published in the following
collections:

The Hawk in the Rain (Faber and Faber, 1957): Macaw and Little
Miss; Meeting.

Lupercal (Faber and Faber, 1960): The Bull Moses; Bullfrog.

Crow (Faber and Faber, 1970): Crow and the Birds.

Season Songs (Faber and Faber, 1976): A March Calf; A Swallow;
Pets; Mackerel Song; Sheep; Starlings Have Come; A Cranefly in
September; Evening Thrush.

Moon-bells (Chatto & Windus, 1978): Tigress; Off-days; Birth of
Rainbow (also in *Moortown*); A Mountain Lion; Coming down
through Somerset (also in *Moortown*); Roe Deer (also in
Moortown).

Remains of Elmet (Faber and Faber, 1979): The Canal's Drowning
Black; The Long Tunnel Ceiling; The Weasels We Smoked out of
the Bank; Curlews (under the titles 'Curlews Lift' and 'Curlews
in April').

Moortown (Faber and Faber, 1979; these poems later included in
Moortown Diary, Faber and Faber, 1989): Teaching a Dumb Calf;
Feeding Out-wintering Cattle at Twilight; Bringing in New
Couples; Struggle; Dehorning; While She Chews Sideways;
Couples under Cover; Happy Calf; February 17th.

Under the North Star (Faber and Faber, 1981): Mosquito.

River (Faber and Faber, 1983): Visitation; Under the Hill of
Centurions; Stealing Trout on a May Morning; Caddis;
Strangers; The Bear; Performance; September Salmon; A Rival;
Whiteness; The Kingfisher; An Eel; The Mayfly is Frail; A
Cormorant.

Flowers and Insects (Faber and Faber, 1986): Eclipse; Where I Sit
Writing My Letter; Tern; Two Tortoiseshell Butterflies; Nightjar.

Wolfwatching (Faber and Faber, 1989): A Macaw; Manchester
Skytrain.

Uncollected: Waterlicked; Sparrow; Cuckoo; Song against the
White Owl; Swans; Black-Back Gull; Shrike; Snipe; Live Skull;
Nightingale; Magpie; Pheasant; Irish Elk; Very New Foal; Buzz
in the Window; Tiger.

Index of First Lines

Of the main road canal bridge 21

Rama, in a horned blood-mask 67
Ran along the rowan branch, a whole family 60
Remember that nightmare straight into the camera 101
Right from the start he is dressed in his best – his blacks and his
    whites 1

She came in reluctant. The dark shed 24
She grin-lifts 9
She is struggling through grass-mesh – not flying 84
Sorcerer! How you hate it all! 77
Struggle-drudge – with the ideas of a crocodile 48
Suddenly hooligan baby starlings 44

The breaker humps its green glass 88
The cormorant, commissar of the hard sea 74
The day darkened in rain. In the bottom of the gorge 64
The ewes are in the shed 80
The Kingfisher perches. He studies 92
The licensed clown – chak chak! 63
The moorland mother's 75
The river is in a resurrection fever 29
The sheep has stopped crying 15
The strange part is his head. Her head. The strangely ripened 93
The strike drags on. With the other idle hands 20
The talons close amicably 47
The tree creeps on its knees 100
The way the shivering Northern Lights are frail 95
The white owl got its proof weapons 23
The wind is inside the hill 36
They lift 79
This crack-brained African priest creates his own temple ruins 54
This morning blue vast clarity of March sky 86
Tide sighs and turns over. The black-backed gull 38
To get into life 14

Walks the river at dawn 78
Washed in Arctic 35
We had been expecting her to calve 49
When the eagle soared clear through a dawn distilling of
    emerald 112

While others sing the mackerel's armour 8
Wind out of freezing Europe. A mean snow 45
With their lithe long strong legs 111

You are soaked with the cold rain 51

Subject Index

This index refers readers to all four volumes of the *Collected Animal Poems*. Numbers in **bold** refer to volume numbers. Individual birds, fish and insects are listed under the category headings BIRDS, FISH and INSECTS.